THE HOLOCAUST
Lost Words

JUDITH SANDEEN BARTEL

The words over the sign of the main gate at Auschwitz translate as "work makes one free", a tragic deception.

KEY TO IMPORTANT ARTICLES

Look out for the following symbols through this book, highlighting key articles from the past.

FILM EXCERPT
Primary source material taken from a film about the subject matter.

SONG EXCERPT
Lyrics extracted from songs about the subject matter.

OFFICIAL SPEECH
Transcribed words from official government speeches.

GOVERNMENT DOCUMENT
Text extracted from an official government document..

LETTER
Text taken from a letter written by a participant in the events.

PLAQUE/INSCRIPTION
Text taken from plaques/monuments erected to remember momentous events described in this book.

INTERVIEW/BOOK EXTRACT
Text from an interview/book by somebody there at the time.

NEWSPAPER ARTICLE
Extracts taken from newspapers of the period.

TELEGRAM
Text taken from a telegram sent to or by a participant in the events.

An Hachette UK Company
www.hachette.co.uk

First published in Great Britain in 2005 by TickTock, a division of Octopus Publishing Group Ltd,
Endeavour House, 189 Shaftesbury Avenue, London, WC2H 8JY.
www.octopusbooks.co.uk

Copyright © Octopus Publishing Group Ltd 2012

ISBN 978 1 84898 692 3

A CIP catalogue record for this book is available from the British Library

Printed in Hong Kong
10 9 8 7 6 5 4

CONTENTS

INTRODUCTION

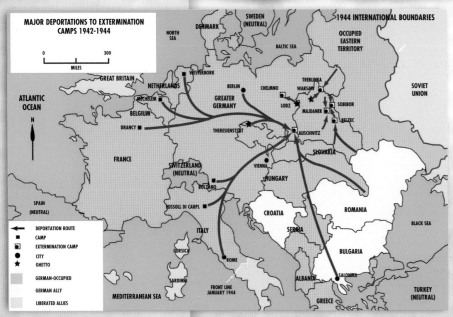

MAJOR DEPORTATIONS TO EXTERMINATION
CAMPS 1942-1944

0   300
MILES

1944 INTERNATIONAL BOUNDARIES

DEPORTATION ROUTE
CAMP
EXTERMINATION CAMP
CITY
GHETTO
GERMAN-OCCUPIED
GERMAN ALLY
LIBERATED ALLIES

Above *A map showing the major extermination camps used during the Holocaust, and the areas where the main deportations took place.*

Below *A map showing the changing Nazi territory during World War II.*

AXIS POWERS, AUGUST 1939
EXTENT OF AXIS CONTROL, MAY 1941
ALLIES
NEUTRAL NATIONS
AXIS OFFENSES
ALLIED OFFENSES
MAJOR BATTLES

*O*ver six million Jews and countless others across Europe were persecuted and murdered systematically by a government-sponsored genocide between 1941-1945. By 1945, two out of every three Jews in the continent had died from over work, starvation, exposure to the elements, bullets, fire, poisonous gas, beatings and the hangman's noose. Every Jewish person living in Europe was a target for extermination by the Nazis. The perpetrators who carried out this massacre of the innocent were scientists, doctors, military and government personnel, and ordinary citizens. This frightening event became known as the Holocaust.

Right *When Adolf Hitler was elected to power in Germany, he quickly unleashed a frightening campaign of persecution against the Jewish people of Europe.*

After World War I, a defeated Germany fell into a social and economic depression. The settlement imposed upon Germany by the victorious Allies after the war, the Treaty of Versailles, forced the Germans to pay compensation and to take the blame for the conflict. Unemployment soared, inflation made the German currency worthless, and a new government called the Weimar Republic was struggling to maintain democracy.

Adolf Hitler, a corporal in the German army became intrigued with the National Socialist People's Party (the Nazis), when he was hired by the German military to spy on them in 1919. Upon their invitation, he became the leader of the Nazi Party. Hitler was a powerful speaker, who gained wide support from the public, with his dramatic speeches and theatrics.

Hitler was legally appointed Chancellor – leader of Germany – in January 1933. The first concentration camp, for political dissenters and communists, opened at Dachau two months later.

Hitler and his corps of terrifying *Sturmabteilung* (SA) soldiers (also known as brownshirts) used fear and violence to manipulate the German people and take complete control of the government. Political opponents and any other people who spoke out against the Nazi regime were silenced by Germany's new Chancellor through his protective police the *Schutzstaffel* (SS), and the *Geheime Staatzpolizei* (Gestapo - the Secret State Police) using extreme violence. Anyone who was identified as an opponent or enemy (Communist,

Above *An emaciated survivor greets United States soldiers at the Buchenwald Concentration Camp on April 18th, 1945.*

Socialist, or trade union leader) was arrested, taken to a work camp, beaten or even killed. The Weimar Republic was dead and Hitler was in complete control.

Hitler had been a racist long before he became Chancellor. He believed there existed a "master" race of physically fit, racially pure people called Aryans, and he saw this group as the future of Germany and all of Europe. His plan to "purify" Germany became a major part of the Nazi plan. Hitler believed that it was critical to open up *Lebensraum* (living space) for the Aryan people in other European countries. In order to accomplish his goal, all people deemed inferior had to be removed. German physicians were bound by law to sterilize anyone who was determined to be inferior, including those who were mentally or physically handicapped, bi-racial, and ethnic minorities such as the Roma, or Gypsy people. These sterilizations were the Nazis insurance that "inferior" people would not reproduce.

Hitler and other Nazi leaders considered the Jewish "race" a danger to the future of Germany. Thousands of years of anti-Semitism had created a history of prejudicial behaviour towards Jews. Hitler's Nuremberg Race laws defined Jewish people not as a religious group, but as a race. Hitler claimed that the Jews were "parasites" who fed off of a host race and weakened them. It was the Jew, Hitler claimed, who was responsible for all that ailed German society. As in the past, Jews became the scapegoat in Germany and other European countries.

Below *A postcard written by a Jewish prisoner of the Auschwitz-Birkenau concentration camp. Most of these postcards were never delivered.*

Prejudicial laws were put in place which forbade Jews from owning businesses, practicing professions, owning property, and even going to public school. After the Germans invaded Poland in 1939, starting World War II, the Jews were forced from their homes into ghettos. Conditions were dreadful; several families living in one room, with only the bare essentials to survive.

Children could not go to school, ride bicycles, and had to surrender their family pets. All valuables had to be turned over to the Nazis. Many people died in the ghettos of disease and malnutrition. As the ghettos became overcrowded, Jews were transported by railroad to concentration camps in Eastern Europe.

As World War II progressed, the Wehrmacht – the German army – marched across Europe. The *Einsatzgruppen* (mobile killing squads) followed in their path executing entire villages of Jews and either burying or burning the bodies in mass graves. Hitler's "Final Solution" was coming to fruition. The *Einsatzgruppen* were not the fastest nor most efficient way to murder, so the Nazis planned and built extermination camps. As the Allied troops closed in on the Nazis, prisoners were sent on "death marches" of several hundred miles only to be executed upon their arrival at the death camps.

In January of 1945 the first Russian troops discovered the camps. Many prisoners continued to die even after the liberation of the camps. The survivors had the difficult and disheartening task of searching for loved ones. With their homes, families and livelihoods gone, many spent years in displaced persons camps before attempting to resume their existence. This is the story of the Holocaust. This is a story that must be told and must be remembered.

Left During Hitler's reign, the Jewish people were forced to wear the Star of David like this button (left) to identify themselves.

Left An Auschwitz survivor holds up his arm to show the tattoo of his number given to him during his imprisonment at the camp.

ATLANTIC
OCEAN

- - - 1914 BOUNDARIES
☐ NEW NATIONS
☐ PLEBISCITE AREAS
☐ OCCUPIED AREA

Above A map of Europe after the Treaty of Versailles. Under its terms, Germany lost territory and suffered humiliation.

"He had lost his leg on the battlefront, and he refused to try to use a wooden leg. Instead he rolled around the house in his wheelchair and stormed at the "bureaucrats and bloodsuckers" who had brought Germany to disgrace. He described leaders of the civilian government as traitors, to whom we owe no loyalty or allegiance. When I brought home the black, red, and gold flag of the new republic (the old flag had been black, white and red), he ripped it up, spat on it, slapped me in the face and told me never to bring that rag into the house again."

Interview with the son of Johann Herbert, conducted in 1951 and later published in 1977.

Before 1914, Germany was the industrial powerhouse of Europe. The military was well-equipped with a strong land army and thriving navy. Germans held great pride in their writers, artists and composers. The school system was world class, and most Germans received an excellent education. Although Germany ended World War I financially better off than most European countries, the defeat caused resentment and a bitterness that would undermine the new democracy formed in 1919.

THE GREAT WAR
On June 28, 1914, World War I began after the heir to the Austro-Hungarian throne, Archduke Franz Ferdinand and his wife were gunned down by a young Serbian terrorist. As a result of Austria-Hungary's declaration of war on Serbia, Russia mobilized against Austria-Hungary. Germany, a member of an alliance with Austria-Hungary and Italy known as the Central Powers, declared war against Russia and France. As a result of Germany's invasion of Belgium, Great Britain mobilized against Germany and Austria-Hungary. World War I raged in Europe for over four years.

Right *Kaiser Wilhelm II of Germany took the country into the First World War.*

Left Despite Germany's airpower – its Fokker Eindecker fighter planes were among the deadliest in the skies – the country was forced to surrender on 11th November, 1918.

JUNE, 1914
Archduke Ferdinand assassinated.

JULY, 1914
Germany pledges support to Austria and Austria declares war on Serbia.

AUG, 1914
The major European powers divide into sides. Hitler joins the German Army.

NOV, 1918
Germany signs armistice with Allies and the war ends.

JUNE, 1919
Treaty of Versailles signed.

On November 11, 1918, a peace agreement was agreed upon between Germany and the Allies-Great Britain, France, the United States and Italy. Germany's defeat in the war spelled the end of its monarchy, and in January 1919, an era of democracy began. A democratic constitution was signed in the city of Weimar, ushering in elections and the era of the Weimar Republic that was to last until 1933. In the summer of 1919, the victorious Allies assembled at Versailles, France to draw up a peace treaty. Initially Germany refused to sign the treaty, but was told that failure to sign would reignite the war.

The admission of blame and financial responsibility for the War caused immediate humiliation, but eventually the treaty increased nationalistic feelings in Germany.

HITLER'S ORIGINS
Adolf Hitler was born on April 20, 1889 in a small Austrian village. After the death of his beloved mother when he was a young adult, Hitler moved to Vienna and lived the life of a recluse for several years. Vienna's mayor, Karl Lueger, captured Hitler's attention and admiration with his charismatic anti-Jewish speeches. When World War I broke out in 1914, Hitler joined the German army. Hitler was particularly

Above *The Hall of Mirrors at the Palace of Versailles, the room where the peace treaty was signed.*

"The Allied and Associated Governments affirm and Germany accepts the responsibility of Germany and her allies for causing all the loss and damage to which the Allied and Associated Governments and their nationals have been subjected as a consequence of the war imposed upon them by the aggression of Germany and her allies. The Allied and Associated Governments, however, require, and Germany undertakes, that she will make compensation for all damage done to the civilian population of the Allied and Associated Powers and to their property during the period of the belligerency of each as an Allied or Associated Power against Germany by such aggression by land, by sea and from the air, and in general all damage as defined in Annex I hereto."

Treaty of Versailles
Part VIII. Reparation.
Section I. General provisions. Article 231.

Above *Map showing the Jewish population of Europe before the Holocaust.*

Above *A photograph of Adolf Hitler as a young baby.*

"Don't think that one can fight against disease without killing the cause, without exterminating the germ; and don't think that one can fight against racial tuberculosis without taking care that the peoples be freed of the germ of racial tuberculosis. The effect of Judaism will never disappear and the poisoning of the people will not end unless the cause - the Jews - are removed from our presence."

Adolf Hitler, Salzburg, August 7, 1920.

offended by Germany's loss of the war, and blamed the Jews and other minority groups for undermining Germany's efforts. In 1919, Corporal Hitler, who was now an informer for the military, was assigned to spy on an anti-Semitic, pro-military, nationalistic political party called the German Worker's Party. At the meeting Hitler became angered by the suggestion that Bavaria break away from Germany. Hitler ranted and raved in a fifteen-minute nationalistic speech which attracted the attention of the party's leader. Hitler accepted the invitation to join the party and quickly became an active leader of the party, which soon changed its name to the National Socialist German Worker's Party, or Nazi Party for short.

Right *A Polish Rabbi helps a Jewish student with lessons from the Hebrew bible. The boy was later murdered in one of Hitler's death camps.*

HITLER IN PRISON

In a foiled attempt to overthrow the Bavarian government in 1923, Hitler was convicted of high treason and sentenced to prison for five years. During the nine months that he served, Hitler would write out his plan for the future of Germany in his book *Mein Kampf* (My Struggle). Hitler blamed the Weimar Republic, the Communists and the Jews for Germany's loss of World War I and the economic and social troubles that followed.

Above *Hitler (far left) fought in the Bavarian regiment of the German army during World War 1.*

TIMELINE 1919-1926

SEPT, 1919
Hitler attends meeting of German Workers Party.

SPRING, 1920
Party changes name and becomes popularly known as the Nazi party.

1923
Hitler becomes leader of party. In November, the failed Beer Hall Putsch takes place. The Hitler Youth is first formed.

1924
Hitler sent to Landsberg prison for treason. He is released after just 13 months.

1925
Hitler's Mein Kampf is published. The SS (*Schutzstaffel*) – Hitler's personal army – is formed.

1926
The Hitler Youth (*Hitler Jugend*) is reformed.

JEWS IN EUROPE

Jews had lived throughout Europe for over 2,000 years. By the time Hitler came into power in 1933, there were nine million Jews living in some twenty-one European countries. In Eastern Europe, Jews lived mostly in small towns called *shtetls*. In these towns most people spoke Yiddish, a mixture of German and Hebrew, and lived very traditional lives. Many wore traditional black caftans and were devoutly observant of the traditional Jewish Religion. In the large cities of Western Europe, Jews lived side-by-side with non-Jews. Jews adopted the culture of their non-Jewish friends. They dressed and spoke the same. Jews were doctors, lawyers, accountants, teachers and farmers.

"Once, as I was strolling through the inner city, I suddenly encountered an apparition in a black caftan and black hair locks. Is this a Jew? was my first thought. For, to be sure, they had not looked like that in Linz. I observed the man furtively and cautiously, but the longer I stared at this foreign face, scrutinizing feature for feature, the more my first question assumed a new form: is this a German?...the more I saw, the more sharply they became distinguished in my eyes from the rest of humanity... For me this was the time of the greatest spiritual upheaval I have ever had to go through. I had ceased to be a weak-kneed cosmopolitan and become an anti-Semite."

Adolf Hitler, Mein Kampf.

Above *This racist German election poster from 1920 criticises the idea of the pure Aryan marrying a stereotypical Jew.*

BUILD UP RISE OF THE NAZIS

Above *A 1933 election poster in Berlin urging citizens to vote for the joint ticket of Hitler and Hindenburg.*

Above *A poster promoting the Hitler Youth movement. Membership eventually became compulsory.*

"I spoke for thirty minutes, and what before I had simply felt within me, without in any way knowing it, was now proved by reality: I could speak! After thirty minutes the people in the small room were electrified and the enthusiasm was first expressed by the fact that my appeal to the self-sacrifice of those present led to the donation of three hundred marks."

Adolf Hitler,
Mein Kampf.

In the 1930 election, the Nazis received over eighteen percent of the votes and catapulted from the smallest party in Germany to the second largest. In 1932, Hitler ran for president and lost in a run-off vote by only 17%. Despite the loss, Hitler had become very popular. In January 1933, after being badgered incessantly by cabinet members, including his own son, Oskar, the senile President Hindenburg appointed Adolf Hitler Chancellor of Germany. It was thought that by keeping him close, others could keep a watchful eye over the charismatic leader. Adolf Hitler had been grossly underestimated.

PRE-WAR NAZI GERMANY

After the stock market crash in the United States in 1929, Germany's economic problems increased ten-fold.

Left *German children in 1923 playing with money in the streets. Under the Weimar Republic, inflation was such that $1 US was worth 4.2 million Deutschmarks, so money was effectively worthless.*

Businessmen saw profits slip; in many cases companies went bankrupt. By 1932 the number of Germans unemployed had reached a record 6 million. Amazingly, the government actually raised taxes in hope of helping the poor. Hitler's appointment brought an end to the weak Weimar Republic, and to democracy in Germany. After the Reichstag building was set ablaze by an arsonist on February 28, 1933, Hitler declared a national state of emergency. The Decree of the Reich President for the Protection of People and State legalized mass arrests of socialists, Communists and any other opponents of the

Hitler became immersed in the party and even renamed the party the National Socialist German Workers' Party, or Nazi party for short. He also chose the symbol for the party, the swastika. What is now considered a symbol of hate, Hitler remembered as a decoration he had seen as a boy in the monastery where he had attended school.

"In the red we see the social idea of the movement, in the white the national idea, in the swastika the mission to struggle for the victory of Aryan man and at the same time the victory of the idea of creative work, which is eternally anti-Semitic and will always be anti-Semitic."

Adolf Hitler, Mein Kampf.

TIMELINE
1933

JAN 30, 1933
Hitler appointed Chancellor.

FEB 28, 1933
Nazis burn Reichstag building. Emergency powers granted to Hitler.

MARCH 22, 1933
Nazis open Dachau concentration camp near Munich.

MARCH 23, 1933
German Parliament passes Enabling Act giving Hitler dictatorial powers.

Nazi regime. Dachau, the first prison camp for political opponents opened in March of 1933, just two months after Hitler was appointed chancellor.

ANTI-SEMITISM
From 70 B.C.E., when the Roman Consul Pompey the Great insisted that Jews worship Roman Gods, to teenagers drawing swastikas on the walls of a synagogue, anti-Semitism has had a long history. Hatred of the Jews began to become widespread after the death of Jesus in 33 AD. Jews do not share the Christian belief that Jesus was the son of God. Although Jesus' death was ordered by the Romans, not the Jews, many

"By appointing Hitler Chancellor of the Reich you have handed over our sacred German Fatherland to one of the greatest demagogues of all time. I prophesy to you this evil man will plunge our Reich into the abyss and will inflict immeasurable woe on our nation. Future generations will curse you in your grave for this action."

Telegram to Hindenburg from former General Erich Ludendorff

Above *Adolf Hitler with President Paul von Hindenburg during ceremonies in Potsdam in March 1933, marking the reopening of the German parliament.*

Above *These two covers from official Hitler Youth magazines show Nazi expectations for what boys and girls should become. Girls magazines told readers to work hard and look after German men, while boys magazines emphasised adventure and excitement.*

"As a member of the storm troop of the NSDAP I pledge myself to its storm flag: to be always ready to stake life and limb in the struggle for the aims of the movement; to give absolute military obedience to my military superiors and leaders; to bear myself honourably in and out of service; to be always companionable towards other comrades."

This was the pledge taken by members of the SA.

Jesus. Historically, this hatred has resulted in Jews being subjected to many discriminatory laws, particularly in the Christian regions of Europe. Forbidden to own land or businesses across parts of the continent, some Jews became money lenders, leading to the stereotype that Jews are ruthless financiers. Hitler's anti-Semitic views attempted to convince gentiles that the Jews were trying to dominate the world economically and politically. Because Jews were in such a minority, less then 1% of the population of Germany, their quiet voice was barely heard over the boisterous, anti-Semitic propaganda trumpeted by the Nazis.

Christians believe that the Jews were responsible for his crucifixion, resulting in some holding the Jews collectively guilty for the death of

HITLER YOUTH

Adolf Hitler's plan was to produce a military and social structure that would support his ideology for the present and the future. To ensure

Below *A Hitler Youth march taking place in 1938, before the outbreak of World War II.*

loyalty for years to come, the *Hitler Jugend* (Hitler Youth) was created. They mirrored the strengthening Nazi party throughout the 1920s and grew in numbers from just under 1000 in 1923 to over 2.3 million by 1933. Hitler Youth soon engulfed all other children's organizations and included boys and girls from the age of four to eighteen. School schedules were adjusted to include challenging physical fitness regiments, and courses which emphasized the Nazi themes of racial struggle and German pride. Courses like biology were eventually removed from the curriculum. What had been a superb, world class German school system became substandard almost overnight. Children were even encouraged to report family or neighbours who spoke out against the Reich. Walter Hess, a Hitler Youth, was elevated to the status of hero by turning in his father for calling Hitler a crazed maniac. His father was taken to Dachau concentration camp.

PERSECUTION OF THE JEWS

On March 23rd, 1933, the newly elected members of the Reichstag met in the Kroll Opera House in Berlin to consider passing a piece of legislation put forward by Hitler called the Enabling Act. Officially titled the 'Law for Removing the Distress of the People and the Reich' it was effectively a bill to end democracy in Germany and establish the legal dictatorship of Adolf Hitler. Just one week after the Act was passed, a national boycott of Jewish shops and department stores was organized by the Nazis. Propaganda

Left A soldier models the uniform of the SA Brownshirts, who helped the boycott of Jewish shops.

TIMELINE
1933

APRIL 1
Nazis stage boycott of Jewish shops and businesses.

JULY 14
The Nazi Party is declared the only legal party in Germany and strips Jewish immigrants from Poland of their German citizenship.

GERMAN BOYS AND GIRLS!

"We National Socialists carried on our struggle for the sake of the German people and its future. The future of the people is its children — which is you. We thought about you as you fought, risking life and health and all we had to help the swastika to victory. You will be spared what the German people had to experience before 1933.

The fatherland's age of distress is past. The machines are running again, the chimneys are smoking. There is work and food. People are happy again and have found new faith. And all are working in the same direction. The people make up a great community, tied together a million-fold by common blood, and faces its future with heads held high.

You are our young team. You will take the storm flags from our hands and carry them into a happier future.

The doors of school are closing behind you. It has prepared you well. Be glad that the present day demands accomplishment and diligence of you. We Germans will not allow ourselves to be surpassed by any other people in the world. Join the ranks of creative Germans, build the new Reich, and be loyal to your last breath."

"You and Your People", from Reichswalter des NSLB (the Nazi organization for teachers), 1940.

Above *Storm Troopers carry piles of books out of a Berlin library to be burnt.*

Above *Works by writers and academics including Sigmund Freud, the "father" of modern psychoanalytic theory, were banned by Hitler.*

Minister Joseph Goebbels urged the boycott of Jewish-owned businesses as a legitimate response to "anti-German atrocity propaganda" carried out by "international Jewry". The Nazis believed that the stories of Germany's atrocities during World War I were being spread by newspapers that the Jews "secretly controlled". Brownshirts stood in the doorways of Jewish-owned stores and encouraged Germans to "defend yourselves against the Jewish atrocity propaganda."

Above *The Nuremburg Race Laws required Jews to identify themselves by wearing a Star of David badge.*

BOOK BURNINGS

On May 10, 1933, students, accompanied by Storm Troopers, made heaping piles of 20,000 books written by Jews or those containing ideas deemed to be "unGerman", poured petrol on them and set them ablaze. Authors like Albert Einstein, Sigmund Freud and Ernest Hemingway, were included in the inferno. Teachers were under constant scrutiny by the Hitler Youth during lessons, and also faced mandatory background checks from Nazi officials to prove the purity of their genealogy. Teachers complained that the new education program did not give students the standard of education they had previously enjoyed, but that did not matter to Hitler.

"My program for educating youth is hard. Weakness must be hammered away. In my castles of the Teutonic Order a youth will grow up before which the world will tremble. I want a brutal, domineering, fearless, cruel youth. Youth must be all that. It must bear pain. There must be nothing weak and gentle about it. The free, splendid beast of prey must once again flash from its eye… That is how I will eradicate thousands of years of human domestication… That is how I will create the New Order."

Adolf Hitler, 1933

"Restrictions on personal liberty, on the right of free expression of opinion, including freedom of the press; on the rights of assembly and association; and violations of the privacy of postal, telegraphic and telephonic communications and warrants for house searches, orders for confiscations as well as restrictions on property, are also permissible beyond the legal limits otherwise prescribed."

The 1933 Emergency Decree

RACE LAWS

Although there are no defining physical or genetic characteristics of all Jews, Hitler claimed that Jews were racially inferior. The Nuremburg Race Laws of 1935 revoked the German citizenship of Jews, and made it illegal for a Jewish person to marry or have sexual relationships with a non-Jewish German. These laws also defined a "Jew" as a person who has three or four Jewish grandparents. The significance of this law was that Judaism was now viewed as a race and not a religion, in that a person cannot change or renounce one's race. People who had converted to Christianity – even priests and nuns – were now considered by law to be Jewish.

Left *Joseph Goebbels was the Reich Minister for Public Enlightenment and Propaganda, which gave him total control of all the German media and the arts.*

TIMELINE 1934-1938

AUG 2, 1934
German President von Hindenburg dies. Hitler becomes *Führer* (leader).

SEPT 15, 1935
Nuremberg Race Laws decreed.

MARCH 12/13, 1938
Annexation of Austria.

JULY, 1938
Evian Conference, France, the U.S. convenes a League of Nations conference with delegates from 32 countries to consider helping Jews fleeing Hitler, but results in inaction as no country will accept them.

JULY 25, 1938
Jewish doctors prohibited by law from practicing medicine.

OCT 5, 1938
Law requires Jewish passports to be stamped with a large red "J".

"The era of extreme Jewish intellectualism is now at an end... The future German man will not just be a man of books, but a man of character. It is to this end that we want to educate you. As a young person, to already have the courage to face the pitiless glare, to overcome the fear of death, and to regain respect for death - this is the task of this young generation. And thus you do well in this midnight hour to commit to the flames the evil spirit of the past. This is a strong, great and symbolic deed - a deed which should document the following for the world to know - here the intellectual foundation of the November (Democratic) Republic is sinking to the ground, but from this wreckage the phoenix of a new spirit will triumphantly rise..."

Propaganda Minister Joseph Goebbels (left), Berlin 1933.

THE CRISIS DEEPENS INTO WAR

LATVIA
LITHUANIA
BALTIC SEA
KOVNO
VILNA
KOENIGSBERG
DANZIG
EAST PRUSSIA
MINSK
GRODNO
NAREW
BIALYSTOK
BERLIN
GREATER GERMANY
POZNAN
WARTA
WARSAW
VISTULA
LODZ
BREST-LITOVSK
KOVEL
LUBLIN
POLAND
PROTECTORATE OF BOHEMIA AND MORAVIA
KRAKOW
LVOV
SLOVAKIA
HUNGARY
ROMANIA
SOVIET UNION

GERMAN FORCES INVADED POLAND SEPTEMBER 1, 1939

SOVIET UNION OCCUPIED EASTERN POLAND SEPTEMBER 7, 1939

Above A map showing the successful German invasion of Poland in September 1939.

O n November 7, 1938, Ernst vom Rath, a German diplomat, was shot in the German Embassy in Paris by Herschel Grynszpan, a 17-year-old Polish-Jewish refugee. Grynszpan had received a message that his family had been expelled from Germany and deported to a refugee camp on the Polish-German border. When vom Rath died two days later, the Nazis unleashed the largest campaign of violence against the German Jews up to this point.

Above A Jewish shop owner in Berlin clears up after Kristallnacht.

NIGHT OF BROKEN GLASS

Kristallnacht ("Night of Broken Glass") is the name given to the violent anti-Jewish action unleashed on German Jews on November 9 and 10, 1938. On this night 7,500 Jewish homes and businesses, and 267 synagogues were vandalized or destroyed by fire. Over 30,000 Jews were taken to concentration camps, and 36 Jews were killed. Afterwards, despite the fact that Jews were the victims of this violence and destruction, the Jewish community was fined 1,000,000,000 Reichsmarks. On November 12, 1938, a law was passed that prevented Jewish businesses from re-opening; placed a curfew on all Jews, and excluded Jews from many public places

"The terrifying happenings of this ghoulish night, the *Kristallnacht*, are considered to be the prelude to the Holocaust. The SS began picking up Jewish families from their homes and were sending them to one of the numerous concentration camps that had sprung up like mushrooms all over Germany and Austria.
But as Hitler had experienced in previous incidents, no world government lodged any serious condemnation strong enough to cause him concern."
"An Unbroken Chain" written by Holocaust survivor Henry Oertelt.

Above Hitler forced all Jews to move into contained areas called ghettos, usually based in the poorest part of towns.

including schools. Newspapers around the world reported this violation of human rights, yet no action was taken.

NAZIS MARCH ON

In the summer of 1938, 32 delegates from countries around the world, including the United States and Great Britain, joined Germany in Evian, France, to discuss the "Jewish problem". All countries showed disdain for Germany's treatment of Jews, yet refused to relax immigration policies so that Jews could leave Germany. It was apparent to Hitler that other countries would not interfere with his plan to cleanse Germany of all her Jews. It was Hitler's quest for *Lebensraum* (living space for Aryans) that influenced the invasion of Poland in September of 1939. Within weeks, the Polish army was defeated and the people were at the mercy of the Nazi forces. The Nazis kidnapped Polish children who had Aryan characteristics, and sent them to be raised by Germans. Polish leaders were shot, while many Poles were relocated so that German families could settle on the most prosperous plots of land.

RELOCATION OF THE JEWS

As the Nazis marched across Eastern Europe, the Germans controlled and contained the Jews by condensing them in small sections of towns and cities, called ghettos. People were only allowed to bring necessities such as one change of clothing and bedding, and were

Above *Life in the Kovno ghetto.*

Below *An illustration entitled "All is well at school now the Jews have gone". Hitler is shown leading Jewish children away from school while Aryan Germans cheer.*

TIMELINE
1938-1939

NOV 9/10TH, 1938
Kristallnacht – The Night of Broken Glass. Nazis later fine Jews for damages related to *Kristallnacht*.

SEPT 1, 1939
Nazis invade Poland. Jews in Germany are forbidden to be outdoors after 8 p.m. in winter and 9 p.m. in summer.

MEASURES AGAINST JEWS TONIGHT.

a) Only such measures may be taken which do not jeopardize German life or property.
b) Business establishments and homes of Jews may be destroyed but not looted.
c) In business streets special care is to be taken that non-Jewish establishments will be safeguarded.

After arrests have been carried out the appropriate concentration camp is to be contacted with a view to a quick transfer...

Message from SS-Grupenführer Heydrich to all State Police Main Offices and Field Offices, November 10.

Above *Life in the ghettos was one of extreme poverty. This photograph taken in 1941 shows three destitute young children on the pavement in the Warsaw Ghetto.*

"Buses arrive in Hadamar several times a week with a large number of these victims. School children in the neighbourhood know these vehicles and say: "Here comes the murder wagon." ...Old people are saying "on no account will I go into a state hospital! After the feeble-minded, the old will be next in line as useless mouths to feed.."

Letter to Reich Minister of Justice from Roman Catholic Bishop of Limburg, 13 August 1941. Pope John Paul II spoke later of the shame he felt that the Catholic Church kept silent about Nazi atrocities carried out during the war.

given insufficient rations of food. One purpose these ghettos served was to act as holding areas until the people could be transported to death and concentration camps. Many people died of starvation, disease, and exposure to cold. The period of time in the ghetto was one of waiting and uncertainty. Some attempted to keep life as normal as possible, secretly holding classes for children and conducting religious ceremonies. Others looked at this time as one for preparation, as did the people of the Kovno Ghetto in Lithuania. During the three years of living in the Kovno Ghetto, the citizens collected and hid everything from Nazi directives, to sketches and diary entries. After the war, those who survived returned to exhume the historical remains.

DEADLY INTENTIONS

In 1939, Hitler authorized a program of extermination called T-4. This euthanasia program was marketed to the public as being a solution to those who were living a "Life without Hope". Mentally and physically disabled people were sterilized, starved, and killed by lethal injection as early as 1939. In 1940 the first gassings began at an asylum at Grafeneck. Growing awareness and public outcry from churches brought attention to the T-4 program. In August of 1941 Hitler gave the "order" to stop all euthanasia programs, but that was only a ploy to stop the protests. Around 275,000 handicapped people were murdered under this program.

EINSATZGRUPPEN

When the mass murder of Jews began, the crimes were committed by mobile killing squads called *Einsatzgruppen*. These units of between 400 and 500

Above *Jewish women are forced to rebuild a ghetto wall in Kovno after a bombing raid in 1941.*

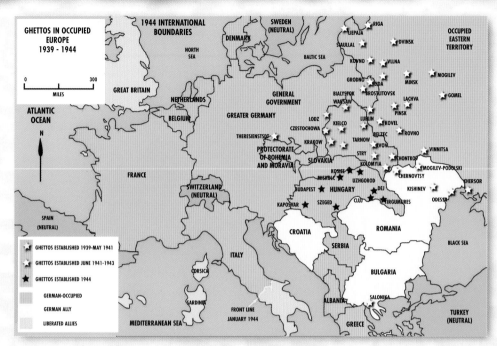

Above *A map showing the main ghettos in Europe between 1939 and 1944.*

GHETTOS IN OCCUPIED EUROPE 1939 - 1944

men followed the Wehrmacht as they invaded Russia in 1941. Their job was to travel from *shtetl* to *shtetl*, collecting valuables, and then murdering the Jewish residents. Sometimes the victims were forced to dig a mass grave before they were shot, other times the bodies were burned on large fire pits. In the town of Ejszyszki, Lithuania, 4,000 Jews were murdered in two days. In 1942 Heinrich Himmler called a halt to this practice because it caused too much emotional stress for the shooters. By the time this practice was stopped, the *Einsatzgruppen* had killed around 1.5 million Jews.

> "We could each pull four or five of the smaller ones (tomatoes) from the vines and place them next to each other onto a piece of torn-off cloth rag. A couple of safety pins secured the ends of the rag inside our pants... Naturally this required some very gingerly walking! Each successful delivery...was a moment of triumph for us."
>
> **"An Unbroken Chain"**
> **written by Holocaust survivor**
> **Henry Oertelt.**

Above *An Einsatzgruppen soldier, part of a mobile killing unit, shoots a Jewish prisoner in Russia, 1941.*

TIMELINE 1939-1940

SEPT 3, 1939
England and France declare war on Germany.

SEPT 27, 1939
Warsaw surrenders. Nazis and Soviets divide up Poland.

OCT, 1939
Nazis begin euthanasia in Germany.

NOV 23, 1939
Yellow stars required to be worn by Polish Jews over age 10.

FEB 12, 1940
First deportation of German Jews into occupied Poland.

APRIL 9, 1940
Nazis invade Denmark and Norway.

> "Above all, we have been put under an obligation to remember, to record events and facts, to describe people and characters, images and important moments; to record in writing, drawing, in painting – in any way available to us."
>
> *Diary entry from Jewish lawyer Avraham Tory, who was held at the Kovno Ghetto.*

Above *The German-born Jew, Anne Frank wrote the most famous diary of the Holocaust whilst in hiding in Holland.*

Above *Two little boys from the Kovno ghetto shown wearing the Star of David.*

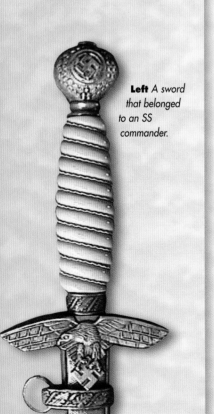

Left *A sword that belonged to an SS commander.*

RESCUE AND RESISTANCE

Resistance to the Nazis was both difficult and dangerous. In Dolhynov, Lithuania, the entire ghetto was murdered when two boys escaped. Despite this, faced with annihilation, millions of persecuted Jews in Nazi Germany and the occupied countries found ways to resist persecution. In occupied countries, thousands of Jews fled to join the Allied fight against the Nazis, while in other cases they formed their own units to wage guerrilla warfare against the Nazis. In Eastern Europe, thousands of Jews banded together in family camps or groups that hid in the forests. They defended themselves with weapons in the face of enemy persecution.

THE WARSAW GHETTO UPRISING

Between 1942 and 1943 underground resistance units had developed in about one-fourth of the ghettos. Because weapons had been confiscated from Jews long before World War II broke out, they had to be smuggled in. The Warsaw Ghetto uprising, led by Mordecai Anielewicz, a Polish Jew, and the Jewish Fighting Organization of Warsaw, was the largest and most symbolic armed revolt against the Nazis. On April 19, 1943, in an attempt to halt deportations from the ghetto, a group of armed men and women attacked the Nazis with hand guns, gasoline grenades and one machine gun. They fought back for almost a month before being defeated. Of the remaining Jews, 56,000 were captured, 7,000 were shot and the rest taken to concentration camps.

CAMP RESISTANCE

Although resistance in the camps meant almost immediate death for prisoners, there were attempts. At Auschwitz, prisoners used gun powder, smuggled in from a munitions factory, to blow up Crematorium IV. At Sobibor extermination camp, 11 SS guards were killed when prisoners revolted. Three hundred escaped, but a third of them were recaptured and executed.

AID FROM OTHERS

Rescue of Jews, although not common, took many forms. Children were hidden in convents, sent to other countries, and hidden in attics and basements. One of the most famous Holocaust victims was a young German girl named Anne Frank. Having fled to Amsterdam, Anne and her family were hidden in an attic apartment behind an office. With the help of Miep Gies, the family hid for two years until the Nazis were tipped off and they were sent to Auschwitz. Anne was then sent to Bergen-Belsen where she died of typhoid.

> "I was 16 at the time and had been in the conspiracy, so to say, for some time. The Germans having closed all the high schools, I participated in classes that met secretly in private homes in groups numbering less than 12. The beginning of the Uprising was greeted with much euphoria. At last we would no longer allow ourselves to be slaughtered like sheep. It was high time to say "enough."
>
> *The recollections of Witold Górski, who fought in the Warsaw Uprising.*

Above: Frightened Jewish residents are taken from the Warsaw Ghetto by soldiers after the Jewish uprising.

MAY, 1940
Nazis invade France, Belgium, Holland, and Luxembourg.

JUNE, 1940
Paris, an opponent of the Axis powers, is occupied by the Nazis.

NOV, 1940
Hungary, Romania, and Slovakia become Nazi Allies.

NOV 15, 1940
The Warsaw Ghetto is sealed off.

15.November.1941
Reichskommissar for Ostland
To: Reich Minister for the Occupied Eastern Territories
RE: Execution of Jews

Will you please inform me whether your inquiry of 31st October should be interpreted as a directive to liquidate all the Jews in Ostland? Is this to be done regardless of age, sex, and economic requirements (for instance, the Wehrmacht's demand for skilled workers in the armament industry)? Of course the cleansing of Ostland of Jews is a most important task; its solution, however, must be in accord with the requirements of war production. . .

Loshe
Reichskommissar for Ostland

A letter from a Nazi commander in Ostland seeking clarification as to which Jews should be murdered. ✉

Above Forcing everyone to wear wool uniforms stripped prisoners in camps of their identity.

Above An example of one of the types of currency issued for use by members of the Jewish ghettos.

"One day, the brothers asked Mrs. Nielsen to help them find a fisherman who would take them to Sweden, where they could escape the Nazis...

As soon as she heard the story, she offered to hide the boys in her home while she arranged for a boat which would take them to Sweden... Through the fishermen, the Danish underground learned of Mrs. Nielsen's act, and contacted her... (as she) was ideally placed to act as liaison between them and the underground. She accepted, and over a hundred refugees passed through her home on the way to Sweden during the following weeks."

An account of Swede Ellen Nielsen's efforts to shelter Jewish children during the war, extracted from "Women in the Resistance and in the Holocaust", edited by Vera Laska and published 1983.

CHAPTER 4

CLIMAX & AFTERMATH THE FINAL SOLUTION

Above *The railtrack arriving at what used to be the Treblinka concentration camp.*

In January 1942, an SS official called Reinhard Heydrich gathered together a team of high-ranking Nazis to discuss what should be done about the "Jewish problem". The result of the Wannsee Conference was called the "Final Solution". The Nazis would use the newest technology in poisonous gassing to exterminate all of the Jews, Gypsies and prisoners of war in Europe. The Nazis wasted no time building extermination camps. The main camps were Treblinka, Belzec, Sobibór and Chelmno.

"...and we say that the war will not end as the Jews imagine it will,...but the result of this war will be the complete annihilation of the Jews.

"And the further this war spreads, the further will spread this fight against the world of the (Jew), and they will be used as food for every prison camp... the hour will come when the enemy of all times, or at least of the last thousand years, will have played his part to the end."

Adolph Hitler speaking to a crowd at the Sports Palace in Berlin, 30 January 1942.

LIQUIDATION OF THE GHETTOS

As soon as the Final Solution was put into motion, the Nazis began liquidating ghettos all over Europe. Jews who had been confined to ghettos were rounded up and loaded onto railroad cars. The ghetto was then destroyed, often by setting it ablaze, to insure that there were no Jews hiding. Two hundred people were jammed into each cattle car. Forced to stand, often for days, they travelled without food, water or bathroom facilities. In the summer people died from heat exhaustion, in the winter many froze to death. The weak often did not survive the trip to the camps.

CAMP SELECTION

Upon arrival at Auschwitz, men and women were separated into two lines. Most young children and elderly people were immediately sent to the gas chamber. Women who refused to give up their babies or were pregnant were sent to the gas chamber with the children. Mothers were forced to make the unthinkable decision of giving up young children to go to the gas chambers with the elderly. Disguised as shower rooms, prisoners were told to place any valuables in piles, and to carefully fold their clothing or hang it on a hook, as they would be returning after taking a shower. Prisoners were given this information so that they would not panic and so they would proceed in an orderly fashion into the gas chamber. Once in the "shower room", which could hold as many as two thousand people in some camps, the doors were closed and the Zyklon-B pellets were dropped down a shoot from the roof. Creating a gas when exposed to air, it took 20–30 minutes for all of the people to die from the poison. The bodies were then removed and burned in crematorium ovens or on large open–air fire pits. In Auschwitz alone, approximately one million people died in the gas chambers.

Above *Jews are unloaded from railroad cars upon arriving at Auschwitz.*

FILM EXCERPT   GOVERNMENT DOCUMENT   INTERVIEW/BOOK EXTRACT   SONG EXCERPT

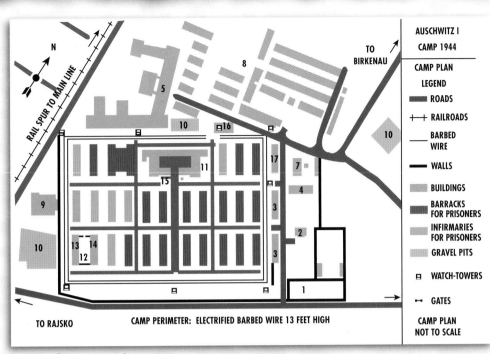

Top *Plan of Camp 1 at Auschwitz 1.*

AUSCHWITZ I
CAMP 1944

CAMP PLAN
LEGEND

▬▬▬ ROADS
+-+-+ RAILROADS
——— BARBED
      WIRE
▬▬▬ WALLS
░░░ BUILDINGS
███ BARRACKS
      FOR PRISONERS
▒▒▒ INFIRMARIES
      FOR PRISONERS
░░░ GRAVEL PITS
⊡ WATCH-TOWERS
⊢⊣ GATES

CAMP PLAN
NOT TO SCALE

TO BIRKENAU

N

RAIL SPUR TO MAIN LINE

TO RAJSKO   CAMP PERIMETER: ELECTRIFIED BARBED WIRE 13 FEET HIGH

SURVIVING SELECTION

Those who were deemed strong enough to work were herded into another building where they were stripped of their identities by having their hair shaved. Prisoners were forced to wear ill-fitting uniforms. By having numbers either sewn on the uniform or tattooed on the forearm, their names were also

Above *Birkenau main gate and guard tower (viewed from inside the camp). The rail line leading into the camp, and all inmates, passed under the archway.*

Above *This photograph shows Jews from Carpatho-Ruthenia at Auschwitz during June 1944 passed fit for work after delousing and head-shaving. This was part of the "registration" process at the camp. The photograph was taken by SS guards for reasons which are still not known.*

TIMELINE
1941

MARCH 1, 1941
Himmler orders a second camp to be built at Auschwitz.

APRIL 6, 1941
Nazis invade Yugoslavia.

JUNE 22, 1941
Nazis invade the Soviet Union.

JULY 31, 1941
Göring instructs Heydrich to prepare for Final Solution.

SEPT 1, 1941
German Jews ordered to wear yellow stars.

"Our poorly lit train station… bustling with noise and commotion… Everyone knew what this meant. They had come to liquidate our ghetto. The Market Square "selections" came first. They forced every man, woman, and child to walk in front of a Gestapo officer. After a quick inspection, he would decide who went to the right, who went to the left. They would keep a small group of young, strong men and women for slave labor. The armed Nazis, their helpers, and the frightening dogs would lead the rest of the people to the railroad station. They would pack them into the waiting cattle cars and send them off to the gas chambers of Treblinka."

Sabina Zimering, from her book Hiding in the Open.

"I remember a very sad day, when six of my friends were hanged by the SS. During all my time in the camps, I have seen maybe 10 executions by hanging. But these six friends… We shared everything we could find in the kommando. It was very difficult to enter in the camp with food because, each time, we were searched by the guards. And if they found something on you, you were immediately hanged. One day, one of these friends had been searched and the SS found a piece of bread in his pocket. The SS said he had stolen it but, in fact, he had received it from a French worker. The next day, the SS hanged my friend; a public hanging. It was horrible for me."

Richard Sufit, interned in Drancy (France) then to Auschwitz-Birkenau on June 30th, 1944.

Below *If a prisoner escaped, other prisoners were held responsible and hanged or shot. These prisoners at Auschwitz are being tortured by sadistic guards in 1944.*

Above *Working in a quarry was quite common work for prisoners. Guards were known to push workers off the quarry walls to their death for pure entertainment. This image shows workers at Auschwitz.*

stripped from them. Tattooing was done only at the Auschwitz camps. Prisoners lived in barracks with hundreds of others and were sent to perform slave labour in quarries or for factories and businesses that helped the Nazi war effort. In most barracks there were no toilets, only a row of buckets with no privacy. Prisoners slept on bunks made of wooden planks, often sleeping five or six to a bunk. Food was scarce and insufficient.

Watery soup made with a piece of rotten vegetable, a small piece of bread and weak coffee was most common. Because people were so dehydrated and malnourished, they often became ill and died of disease. One of the most dreaded events was roll call. Those who collapsed were shot on the spot or sent to the gas chambers.

SONDERKOMMANDO

The Nazis committed many atrocious acts, but one of the most sadistic punishments for prisoners was to be assigned to the *Sonderkommando*. These Jewish prisoners were forced to perform the "dirty work" for the Nazis. One group was responsible for meeting the trains and deceiving the new arrivals into believing that they were being deloused and disinfected when they were actually going to their death. Sometimes members of the *Sonderkommando* knew the people going to the gas chambers. Other teams processed the corpses after the gas chambers. Gold teeth were extracted, clothing and valuables were removed, and bodies were cremated. The warehouse in which valuables were stored was called "Kanada" because it was thought that Canada was a country of great, undiscovered treasure. Although the *Sonderkommando* had better living conditions – decent food and normal clothing – their life expectancy was only several months. The Nazis did not want any witnesses, so every few months all of the *Sonderkommando* were gassed. Other prisoners regarded the *Sonderkommandos* with contempt.

Above *Gold teeth extracted from corpses at Auschwitz.*

Author Primo Levi described them as being "akin to collaborators." For this reason, some entered the gas chambers of their own free will rather than having to perform the grizzly tasks assigned. The *Sonderkommando* at Birkenau organized an uprising that took place on October 7, 1944. Aided by women from the Monowitz camp, who worked in a munitions factory,

TIMELINE
1941-1942

SEPT 17, 1941
Beginning of general deportation of German Jews.

DEC 7, 1941
Japanese attack Pearl Harbor. The next day the United States and Britain declare war on Japan.

JAN 20, 1942
Wannsee Conference to coordinate the "Final Solution".

DEC 10, 1942
The first trains carrying Jews from Germany arrive at Auschwitz.

"They were taken by groups into a big room which looked exactly like a shower room, but when the room was filled with prisoners the doors were closed and the gas Zyklon-B was released through holes in the floor and ceiling. In about ten minutes all who were in the room would be dead. A special kommando called the *Sonderkommando*, consisting of about eight hundred strong young Jewish prisoners selected from the Jewish transports, transferred the corpses from the gas chambers to the crematoria."

Petro Mirchuk,
Ukranian Jew testifies as
to what happened
in Auschwitz.

Above *This photograph was taken in 1944 by a camp inmate at Birkenau assigned to one of the special prisoner teams (Sonderkommando) who were forced to work in the gas chamber or crematoria. This photo shows prisoners burning naked corpses freshly removed from the gassing facility at Crematorium-V.*

> "He grabbed her by the neck and proceeded to beat her head to a bloody pulp. He hit her, slapped her, boxed her, always her head - screaming at the top of his voice, "You want to escape, don't you. You can't escape now. You are going to burn like the others, you are going to croak, you dirty Jew." As I watched, I saw her two beautiful, intelligent eyes disappear under a layer of blood. And in a few seconds, her straight, pointed nose was a flat, broken, bleeding mass. Half an hour later, Dr. Mengele returned to the hospital. He took a piece of perfumed soap out of his bag and, whistling gaily with a smile of deep satisfaction on his face, he began to wash his hands."
>
> **Dr. Gisella Perl,**
> **inmate at Auschwitz.**

Below *Josef Mengele, the "Angel of Death".*

Above *Both Jewish and gypsy children were the victims of Josef Mengele, the "Angel of Death". Twins especially were subjected to painful grotesque experiments. This photograph shows children who survived at Auschwitz.*

gunpowder was smuggled to the *Sonderkommando* at Birkenau. One of the gas chambers was destroyed, but all participants of the uprising died in the explosion and its aftermath.

MEDICAL EXPERIMENTS

The 200 Nazi doctors stationed at some camps performed selections and medical experiments. The medical experiments fell into three categories: those designed with medical objectives in mind to aid the Reich personnel; the second was to aid pharmaceutical companies with research on drugs and treatment of disease; and thirdly those which were designed to help the Nazis develop a pure Aryan race. What these experiments had in common was that they defied any moral and ethical responsibility on the part of the physician. The survival and rescue experiments were designed to discover the human potential when the body is placed under harsh or stressed conditions. The most infamous doctor was Dr. Josef Mengele, known as the "Angel of Death." Mengele performed his racial experiments at Auschwitz from 1943-1945 mostly on sets of twins and dwarfs. "Mengele's children", as the twins were called, received special treatment initially, but were subjected to a much crueller fate. As part of his racial hygiene theory, children were injected with dye in an attempt to change their eye colour. This often resulted in blindness and death. Twins were given blood transfusions of the wrong blood type, which produced massive headaches, high fever and often death. Other children were subjected to castration, amputation, and other frightening and painful surgical procedures, always performed without the use of anesthetic.

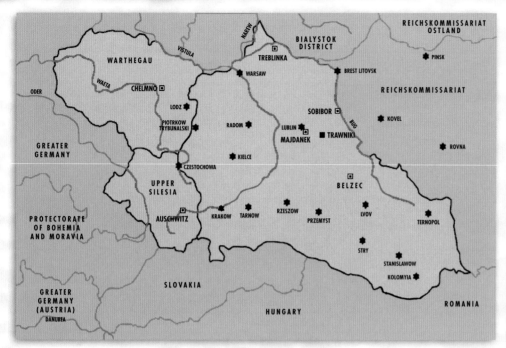

Above *Map showing the location of the main extermination camps built as part of the "Final Solution".*

JULY 9/10, 1943
Allies land in Sicily.

AUG 2, 1943
200 Jews escape from Treblinka extermination camp, only to be hunted down by the Nazis one by one.

NOV 4, 1943
Nazi newspaper Der Stürmer, claims that Jews have now disappeared from Europe.

MARCH 24, 1944
President Roosevelt issues a statement condemning German and Japanese ongoing "crimes against humanity".

JUNE 6, 1944
D-Day: Allied landings in Normandy.

JUNE-JULY, 1944
The New York Times reports via the London Daily Telegraph that over 1,000,000 Jews have already been killed by Nazis.

EXTERMINATION CAMPS

Extermination camps, or killing centres, were designed for instant and secret death. There were six killing centres all located in rural Poland. The first extermination camp, Chelmno, 45 miles from Lodz in western Poland, opened in December of 1941. There, mobile gas vans were used to kill mostly Jews and some Gypsies. With the verbal directive of the Final Solution, Hitler and Himmler set about to create Operation Reinhard - a scheme to exterminate the Jewish population of Warsaw, Krakow, Lublin, Radom and Lvov. According to the Nazis, these areas were inhabited by over two million Jews. The actual killing was to be carried out in three death camps – Belzec, Sobibór and Treblinka. These three camps were built in secluded areas and used carbon monoxide gas chambers to kill Jews. Under Operation Reinhard, an estimated 1.7 million Jews and 52,000 Gypsies were murdered. There were only 120 known survivors.

Above *Crematorium ovens were used to dispose of dead bodies. Ashes were then placed in urns and buried. Some ash was sold to grieving survivors, who thought that these were the remains of relatives.*

"Werner Rhode hated his work, and Hans König was deeply disgusted by the job... (they) had to get drunk before they appeared on the ramp. Only two doctors performed the selections without any stimulants of any kind: Dr. Josef Mengele and Dr. Fritz Klein. Dr. Mengele was particularly cold and cynical. He (Mengele) once told me that there are only two gifted people in the world, Germans and Jews, and it's a question of who will be superior. So he decided that they had to be destroyed."

Dr. Ella Lingens, an Austrian doctor who was imprisoned at Auschwitz for attempting to hide some Jewish friends, describes how Dr Mengele relished his role as selector.

Above *SS soldiers bury the dead of the Belsen Concentration Camp after the liberation of the camp by the Allies. In the six weeks after the British arrived a further 13,000 camp victims died.*

"By way of the redistribution camp Westerbork, I ended up in Auschwitz… Of the 1,200 people in our transport, 1,000 were gassed to death immediately; 120 men and 60-80 women were allowed to stay alive a little longer. At the time, the average time of survival was three months… Everything was taken away from us, except for a pair of glasses and a belt. Within a few hours, we had been reduced to bald shaven, rag-clad souls identified by number, who from that day on vegetated in a state of complete abandonment, hopelessness, and wretchedness. Our bleak life was full of suffering, disease, hunger, and cold, and was constantly threatened by the gas chamber."

Max Hamburger, a Dutch Jew, writes about his experience at Auschwitz.

OTHER KILLING CENTRES

Initially built for Poles, Polish Jews, and Polish resisters, Majdanek outside Lublin, Poland, was primarily a forced work camp. Due to resistance uprisings in Treblinka and Sobibór, the SS in Berlin decided to kill the remaining Jews in Majdanek. Code named Operation *Erntefest* ("Harvest Festival"), 18,000 Jews were shot while music was played to drown out the sound of gunfire. Auschwitz, located in Poland, was the largest of the German camps, and was a complex including a concentration camp, extermination camp and labour camp. Auschwitz I, a concentration camp used mainly as a prison for political criminals, also had a gas chamber and crematorium. Auschwitz II, or Auschwitz-Birkenau, had the largest number of prisoners, and was constructed when the Nazis realised that Auschwitz I would not be large enough to handle exterminations. Four large crematoriums that included disrobing areas, gas chamber, and ovens were built in Birkenau. Zyklon-B, an insecticide, became the most cost-effective way to gas people at Auschwitz. The largest wave of deportees came from Hungary in 1944. Auschwitz III, called Monowitz, was built for slave labourers so they could work at the Buna synthetic

Above *When Allied troops discovered the first camps, they had no idea what they were seeing. Prisoners at this camp at Buchenwald were so thin from malnutrition that they appeared to be walking corpses.*

Above *Prisoners were forced to sleep as many as three or four to a wooden bunk, stacked four levels high.*

AUG 4, 1944
Anne Frank and family arrested by Gestapo in Amsterdam

AUG 6, 1944
The last Jewish ghetto in Poland, Lodz, is liquidated.

NOV 25, 1944
Himmler orders the destruction of crematories at Auschwitz.

rubber works. There were also a series of sub-camps attached to Auschwitz III. Workers were regularly subjected to the selection process where the sick were sent to the gas chambers at Auschwitz-Birkenau.

LIBERATION
On July 23, 1944 the first Soviet troops stumbled upon Majdandek in Poland. On January 27, 1945 Auschwitz-Birkinau was liberated. The soldiers found hundreds of sick, starving people, half of whom died shortly after the Allies arrived. The Nazis were forced to leave so quickly that they left rooms filled with piles of eye glasses, shoes, gold from human teeth, and many written records of the atrocities that had taken place. Although the Nazis had attempted to blow up the crematorium, there were still people who looked like walking corpses, and piles of dead bodies to tell the story. The first response of the liberators was to give the starving people food. Unfortunately many who had survived the Nazis after because they ate foods that were too rich for

Above *This photo was taken at the former Concentration Camp Buchenwald weeks after the liberation. GIs laid wreaths over piles of dead bodies during visits to the camp.*

Above *Eyeglasses were taken from prisoners upon arrival, because the Nazis planned to sell them.*

"In April 1945, I was freed, more dead than alive, from the Buchenwald Concentration Camp by the 8th American Army under the leadership of General Patton. I was so weak at the time that I could no longer walk. I remember one particular night: I was lying in bed, consumed with fever. The good American food didn't agree with my drained stomach and my weakened bowels, and only increased my exhaustion. I got the feeling that "if I fall asleep now, I won't wake up tomorrow!" At that moment, I decided that I couldn't allow myself to die. If I did, I wouldn't be able to fulfill my assignment: to bear witness to that which had happened to us."

Max Hamburger, Dutch Jew, recalls being liberated by the Allies.

Above Poster advertising the film Der Ewige Jude (The Eternal Jew), shown in 1933. The Nazis used propaganda to portray Jews as vermin infiltrating the sanctity of Aryan life.

> "Propaganda has only one object - to conquer the masses. Every means that furthers this aim is good; every means that hinders it is bad."
>
> **Goebbels diaries, 1929.**

Below Poster showing Hitler as a knight in shining armour leading the Germans into battle and out of despair.

The mere mention of the Holocaust today usually evokes feelings of sorrow for the many lives lost, anger at the perpetrators, and guilt for not having done enough to stop Hitler and the Nazis. The truth of the matter is, many countries knew exactly what was going on in the camps at the time, but anti-Semitic feelings prevailed throughout Europe and the United States. While many posters, speeches, films and books voiced their anti-Semitic feelings loudly, others however refused to be silent about the atrocities committed against European Jews.

PROPAGANDA

One of the Nazis most effective methods for brainwashing people was the use of propaganda.

Hitler himself declared in *Mein Kampf* that propaganda was one of the most effective ways of getting a message across to the German public. Once Hitler was in power he set up the *Reichministerium für Volksaufklärung und Propaganda* (Ministry for Popular Enlightenment and Propaganda) under

Below
Dr. Seuss created the Sneetches to draw attention to anti-Semitism.

Dr Joseph Goebbels. In newspapers, *Der Stürmer*, in particular, anti-Semitic cartoons portrayed Jews as the devil, child killers and molesters of women. In children's books, the young were warned about taking sweets from Jews lest it might be poisoned. Before movies were shown in theatres, anti-Semitic short films, such as *Der Ewige Jude (The Eternal Jew)*, depicted Jews as sub-human rats that infested their host country. Hitler, on the other hand, was depicted as a God-like saviour.

CARTOONS

There were however those who made a mockery of the "silly little man with the moustache". Arthur Szyk, a native Pole living in the United States, unleashed his paint brush against the atrocities of the Nazis and became America's leading political caricaturist during World War II. Arthur Szyk's "A Madman's Dream" depicts Hitler seated on a throne with the world in his lap and a "Jew-skin" rug underneath him. Uncle Sam and John Bull are shown in chains pleading with him. Dr Seuss, known for his tongue-twisting children's books, started his career as a political cartoonist for several different magazines. Theodor ("Ted") Seuss Geisel was born on March 2, 1904, in Springfield, Massachusetts. During World War II, Seuss drew editorial cartoons for the left-wing New York newspaper PM, and made

army propaganda films with Frank Capra. The Sneetches was inspired by Seuss's opposition to anti-Semitism. In the stories, some Sneetches have a green star on their belly, and the presence or absence of these stars is the basis for discrimination.

Below Arthur Szyk's "A Madman's Dream" ridicules Hitler. It depicts him seated on a throne with the world in his lap and a Jewish skin rug underneath him. Uncle Sam and John Bull are shown in chains pleading with him.

> "I had one purpose: I wanted to, wherever I could at this particular time, point out as strongly as I could that the United States was going to get involved in this war."
> **Interview with Dr Seuss, 1976.**

TIMELINE
1945

JAN 6, 1945
Soviets liberate Budapest, freeing over 80,000 Jews.

JAN 17, 1945
Liberation of Warsaw by the Soviets.

JAN 27, 1945
Soviet troops liberate Auschwitz. By this time, an estimated 1,500,000 Jews, have been murdered there.

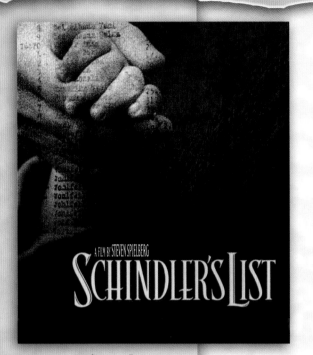

Above A poster from Spielberg's Schindler's List.

Above Set during the Warsaw Ghetto uprising, The Pianist illustrates what life was like for those forced to live in hiding.

At the end of the story the Sneetches learn that neither plain-belly nor star-belly sneetches are superior, and they are able to get along and become friends. The story teaches that all people are the same on the inside, despite outward differences.

THE HOLOCAUST ON FILM

The suffering of the Jewish people in Germany was portrayed on film as early as 1941. Major American film studios refused to portray Hitler in a negative light, but because the English actor Charlie Chaplin produced his own films, *The Great Dictator* was shown in cinemas everywhere. In Chaplin's satire on Nazi Germany, dictator Adenoid Hynkel has a double – a poor Jewish barber – who one day is mistaken for Hynkel. Chaplin later claimed that he never would have made light of the Holocaust had he known the extent of the violence and death. In 1964, Sidney Lumet's *The Pawnbroker*, portrayed a Holocaust

survivor experiencing flashbacks of his time spent in a Nazi camp, but not until 1978 did a film accurately portray the Nazi atrocities. *The Holocaust,* 1978, was a nine-hour mini-series shown on American television. This series prompted discussions about Holocaust history in both the United States and Europe. More recently Steven Spielberg's *Schindler's List*, 1993, has received critical acclaim for the accurate depiction of historical events. Filmed in black and white, Spielberg's academy award-winning film exposed the history of the Holocaust to more people than any other film in the 20th century.

LITERATURE

The Nobel Peace Prize winner Elie Wiesel wrote the book *Night* based on his own experiences in Birkenau, Auschwitz, and Buchenwald. Since its publication, many other

Right Charlie Chaplin starred in several films that poked fun at dictators such as Hitler. Chaplin was hated by the German leader.

"Today is history. Today will be remembered. Years from now the young will ask with wonder about this day. Today is history and you are part of it. Six hundred years ago when elsewhere they were footing the blame for the Black Death, Casimir the Great - so called - told the Jews they could come to Krakow. They came. They trundled their belongings into the city. They settled. They took hold. They prospered in business, science, education, the arts. With nothing they came and with nothing they flourished. For six centuries there has been a Jewish Krakow. By this evening those six centuries will be a rumor. They never happened."

Quote from SS officer Amon Goeth in Steven Spielberg's Schindler's List (1993).

survivors have summoned the courage to relive the past and write their own biographies. In Simon Wiesenthal's *The Sunflower*, a dying Nazi soldier asks for forgiveness from a Jewish prisoner working in the hospital. This book includes responses from prominent 20th century personalities such as the Dalai Lama and Dith Pran, a survivor of the Cambodian killing fields and challenges the reader to ask, "What would you do?" A collection of artwork and poetry created by the children of the Theresien ghetto has also become immortalized in the book *I Never Saw Another Butterfly*.

Above *Survivor Elie Wiesel is a Nobel Peace Prize winner and champion for human rights.*

"First they came for the Jews and I did not speak out – because I was not a Jew.

Then they came for the communists and I did not speak out – because I was not a communist.

Then they came for the trade unionists and I did not speak out – because I was not a trade unionist.

Then they came for me – and there was no one left to speak out for me."

A poem by Pastor Martin Niemoller, Berlin, 1939. Niemoller was a pastor in the German Confessing Church who spent over eight years in a Nazi concentration camp.

TIMELINE
1945-1947

APRIL 23, 1945
Berlin reached by Soviet troops.

APRIL 29, 1945
U.S. 7th Army liberates Dachau.

APRIL 30, 1945
Hitler commits suicide in his bunker.

MAY 7, 1945
Unconditional German surrender signed by General Gustav Jodl, Chief of Staff of the German Army.

OCT 1946
Nuremberg court issues its first verdicts.

MAY 1948
Britain renounces mandate in Palestine, paving the way for the creation of the Jewish state of Israel.

Above *After a ten-year silence, Elie Wiesel wrote the book Night. This book captured the attention of readers everywhere and brought worldwide attention to the Holocaust.*

"The Nazi Holocaust, which engulfed millions of Jews in Europe, proved anew the urgency of the reestablishment of the Jewish State, which would solve the problem of Jewish homelessness by opening the gates to all Jews and lifting the Jewish people to equality in the family of nations...This recognition by the United Nations of the right of the Jewish people to establish their independent State may not be revoked. It is, moreover, the self-evident right of the Jewish people to be a nation, as all other nations, in its own sovereign State."

May 14, 1948, David Ben-Gurion, the chairman of the Jewish Agency for Palestine

A fter the evil perpetrated by the Nazis was finally ended in 1945, it was left to the victorious Allies to try to put together a fair and just settlement. A new Jewish state was created in the Middle East. Israel was to provide a permanent home for Jewish people in the post-Holocaust era, and a symbol of the victorious Allies' commitment that Holocaust should never be allowed to happen again. After the end of the war, there was also the urgent task of bringing those who perpetrated the horrors of the Holocaust to account.

Below *This photograph was used after the war, by a Jewish father in France, in an attempt to locate his four-year old son, Albeit Smiel Vieder. It is likely that many copies of this photo were circulated in France.*

RETURN TO LIFE
After the jubilation and realisation that they were free, survivors faced the task of returning to real life. With mixed emotion, some people searched for loved ones, many of whom, they would discover, had perished. Some returned "home" to find another family living where they used to live, or that their home had been destroyed during the war. During this same year, the United States signed the Displaced Persons Act of 1948. This act allowed for fewer restrictions on immigrants, but it also contained strong anti-Semitic sentiments and restricted the number of Jews allowed to immigrate. Displaced Persons camps were set up to help survivors reunite with family and friends, and readjust to society. There, people waited to be admitted to countries like the United States and the British mandate of Palestine. Under British control, few people were admitted to Palestine without correct documentation.

A NEW STATE IS BORN
To put an end to this scandalous treatment of survivors, in 1947 the United Nations Special Commission on Palestine (UNSCOP)

"I got shipped, um, got shipped to France and finally wound up in a, in an orphanage in Fublaines. It, which is just on the outskirts of Paris. And I was one of the youngest children there, and I didn't speak to anybody except Miriam (a friend of Irene's), who was about, I guess about seven years older. She seemed like almost a mother figure in a sense to me, because she would, I had these long curls and she would fuss with them and she just was very compassionate, and I, um, the other children — I was the only child there with a number, so I also felt that there was something wrong with me. I felt that I had done something horrible, that I had gotten the number and nobody else did. Most of these children had escaped somehow by hiding, or their parents had temporarily given them over and some were subsequently reunited with parents, and some just had family members and they were just waiting to be shipped to, and you know, things like that."

Survivor Irene Hizme describes life in a Catholic orphanage in postwar France in a 1995 interview.

recommended that Palestine be divided into an Arab state and a Jewish state. This was the culmination of a long campaign by Zionists (Jewish nationalists) for an independent Jewish state. However, Zionism was by no means supported by all Jewish people and the foundation of the state of Israel was opposed by the Palestinians and other Arab peoples. Conflict between the two sides has lead to much bloodshed since 1948. The Jews accepted this split, but the Arabs rejected it. The plan was adopted on November 29, 1947, largely due to the support of Harry S. Truman. It soon became painfully obvious that this plan would not work. The Arabs declared war to rid Palestine of Jews. At the end of 1948 ceasefire lines were formally established. The Holy City of Jerusalem was divided into an Israeli part (western) and a part controlled by Jordan (eastern). Jordan's section contained the old walled city which held several important Jewish, Muslim and Christian religious sites.

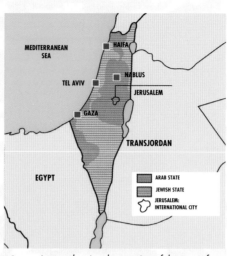

Above *A map showing the creation of the state of Israel as proposed by the UN in 1947.*

Below *A map showing the revised area of Israel after the 1949 conflict.*

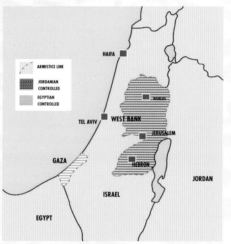

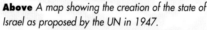

Above *The Nuremburg Trials saw 22 Nazis face accusations of war crimes, but many more escaped justice.*

1948
UN Resolution 181 formally divides Palestine into two, creating the state of Israel.

1949
Israeli-Arab War ends.

1952
Reparations deal signed between West Germany and Israel.

1956
Israel occupies Gaza Strip.

1967
Six Day War begins.

"I have never felt able to describe my emotional reaction when I first came face to face with indisputable evidence of Nazi brutality and ruthless disregard of every shred of decency...I visited every nook and cranny of the camp because I felt it my duty to be in a position from then on to testify at first hand about these things in case there ever grew up at home the belief or assumption that the stories of Nazi brutality were just propaganda."

General Dwight D. Eisenhower, Supreme Commander, Allied Forces, Europe.

Right *Adolf Eichmann shown during his trial for war crimes. He was executed on May 31, 1962.*

When I was maybe seven, eight years old, we had recently moved to Washington and on a hot day, we decided to go to the beach. And people told us that there was a lovely beach somewhere in Chesapeake Bay, and we drove down there. And I still remember the sign, because as we drove up, we saw the sign, which said, "No Jews or dogs allowed."

Ruth Fein, American Jewish Historical Society.

Above *After the war famous artwork and other valuables confiscated by the Nazis were discovered. Here Jewish property stolen by the Nazis is uncovered in Switzerland.*

"There are 350,000 survivors of the Holocaust alive today…There are 350,000 experts who just want to be useful with the remainder of their lives. Please listen to the words and the echoes and the ghosts. And please teach this in your schools."

Steven Spielberg, Academy Award acceptance speech.

A SEARCH FOR JUSTICE

In 1942, long before Adolf Hitler committed suicide in a bunker below Berlin, the Allied powers, including the United States, Great Britain and the Soviet Union, declared the Nazis would be prosecuted for the mass murder of Jews. These trials began in October of 1945 in Nuremberg, Germany. Of the twenty two major Nazi criminals who were tried by the International Military Tribunal, twelve were sentenced to death and seven received prison sentences ranging from ten years to life. Three others were acquitted. The Subsequent Nuremberg Proceedings, as twelve other trials were referred to, involved Gestapo agents, SS men and industrialists who were accused of using slave labour for profit, implementing the Nuremberg Race Laws, medical experimentation and the sale of Zyklon-B. The final defendants, the largest group prosecuted, included camp guards, members of the *Einsatzgruppen*, police officers and doctors who performed medical experiments. Auschwitz had its own tribunal which sentenced its Commandant, Rudolf Höss, to death. Many former Nazis did not receive any sentence at all, however, and returned to normal life in Germany.

NAZI HUNTING

Some Nazis fled to other countries, particularly in South America. Adolf Eichmann, a key figure in the implementation of the "Final Solution", was caught in Buenos Aires, Argentina in May of 1960. Eichmann was caught by the Israeli Security Service and executed after his trial. His sentence marks the only time a prisoner has been put to death in Israel. Nazi hunter and survivor Simon Wiesenthal operates a Nazi documentation centre in Vienna. Klaus Barbie, "the butcher of Lyon", was caught and tried in 1987. He received a life sentence in prison. The "Angel of Death", Dr. Josef Mengele, managed to hide from Nazi hunters until his death from drowning in 1979.

THE US REMEMBERS

In 1978 United States President Jimmy Carter announced the establishment of the President's Commission on the Holocaust. One of its goals was to establish a memorial to Holocaust victims and survivors. In 1993, The United States Holocaust Memorial Museum was opened on Raoul Wallenberg Place in Washington D.C. The museum houses several permanent exhibits including "Remember the Children: Daniel's Story" and "The Holocaust", which spans three floors. The building also contains a research library, two theatres, a Wall of Remembrance and a memorial space for reflection, The Hall of Remembrance.

YAD VASHEM

Established in Jerusalem in 1953, *Yad Vashem* is the Holocaust Martyrs' and Heroes' Remembrance Authority. It is the Jewish people's memorial to those murdered by the Nazis. It contains the world's largest archive of information on the Holocaust – over 63 million pages of documents, almost 300,000 photographs and thousands of films and survivor testimony. *Yad Vashem* also includes several museums, numerous memorials and an International Institute for Holocaust Studies.

HOLOCAUST DENIAL

Despite the extensive documentation, photographs and survivor testimony, there are some people who claim that the Holocaust never occurred. As the survivors have had the courage to tell their stories and as cities throughout the world have established Holocaust museums and memorials, the deniers have also come forward. There is little controversy over the fact that the Nazis hated Jews and discriminated against them; what is being denied is the planned, systematic persecution and murder of six million European Jews. Deniers claim that the film footage, architectural ruins, documents and testimony from survivors and perpetrators is fabricated. Most of this denial comes from those who are anti-Semites masquerading as historians. The rash of deniers and denial groups does not concern serious students and scholars, as the artefacts and the survivors have preserved the truth.

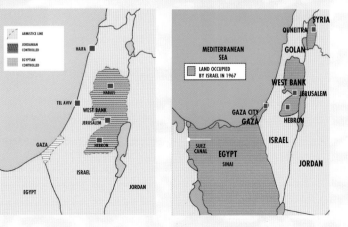

1973
Yom Kippur War starts.

1979
Israel and Egypt sign peace treaty.

1982
Israel invades Lebanon.

1987
Mass Palestinian uprising (*intifada*) against Israeli occupation of Gaza.

1992
Talks in Oslo lead to Declaration of Principles.

2005
The second *intifada* occurs.

2005
The 60th anniversary of the liberation of the extermination and concentration camps.

Left *The United States Holocaust Memorial Museum opened in 1993, and serves as the country's memorial to the millions of people murdered during the Holocaust.*

Left *The map on the left shows the boundaries of Israel before the 1967 war. The next maps shows the boundaries after the conflict. It continues to change.*

The Holocaust was perpetrated by a number of individuals who pursued Hitler's goals with great zeal and in some cases, enjoyment. Many showed no remorse even after the end of the war, and testified at the Nuremburg trials that they believed in what they were doing. On the Jewish side, resistance against this frightening onslaught took many forms. Some people stole food from the Nazis, some kept the Sabbath while others wrote poetry. Some forms of resistance however were more overt, including armed uprisings in the ghettos and Nazi camps.

Adolf Hitler (Nazi) 1889-1945

Adolf Hitler was born on April 20, 1889 in Braunau-am-Inn, Austria. Hitler did not excel at school and left early in the hope of becoming an artist. He fought in a Bavarian regiment during World War 1, and after the war joined the German Workers' Party in 1919 – later to become the Nazi party – and quickly gained total control. Imprisoned after attempting to overthrow the Weimar Republic government, Hitler emerged even more determined in his quest for power. Hitler became Chancellor of Germany in 1933 and abolished democracy soon after. From 1936 onwards he initiated a program of German expansion, and a brutal campaign against the Jewish people of Europe. On 30th April 1945, surrounded by Allied troops, Hitler committed suicide with his wife, Eva Braun, whom he had married the day before.

Reinhard Heydrich (Nazi) 1904-1942

Born in the German city of Halle, near Leipzig on March 7, 1904, Reinhard "the Hangman" Heydrich was responsible for organizing the murder of all the Jewish people of Europe. He was described as someone for whom "truth and goodness had no meaning." Heydrich was also the leader of the *Einsatzgruppen*, and orchestrated the meeting at Wannsee to introduce high ranking Nazis to the "Final Solution". Heydrich was also responsible for organizing the deportation of European Jews to death camps. In 1942 he died from injuries received when a bomb was thrown into his vehicle.

Irma Grese (Nazi) 1923-1945

Born on October 7, 1923, Irma Grese rose to become one of the most notorious female Nazi war criminals. At the age of just 19, Irma became a guard at Ravensbruck and was later transferred to Auschwitz camp. Carrying a whip and a pistol, survivors tell tales of Irma Grese's sadistic treatment of prisoners. She seemed to take delight in the selection process, and the skins of inmates were found in her quarters, having been made into gruesome lamp shades. Irma Grese was found guilty in the Belsen trial, and hung for her crimes.

Heinrich Himmler (Nazi) 1900-1945

Heinrich Himmler was born in Munich on 7 October, 1900. After failing as a poultry farmer, he went on to be appointed Reichmarshal of the *Schutzstaffel*, and became the second most powerful man in Germany. In 1933, Himmler helped to set up the first concentration camp in Dachau, Poland. Himmler also created the *Lebenborn* – "spring of life" – which promoted the "breeding" of Nordic young girls to SS men. After illegitimate children were born, they were given to the SS to raise in the Nazi fashion. After the invasion of Poland this policy changed to include kidnapping children considered to be "racially good". It was also Himmler who came up with the idea of using gas to kill Jews and other prisoners of the Nazis in special chambers disguised as shower rooms. Himmler committed suicide while awaiting trial for war crimes in 1945.

Janusz Korczak (Jewish) 1879-1942

Janusz Korczak, born Henryk Goldsmit, was born in Warsaw in 1879. He established a Jewish orphanage in Warsaw, Poland in 1912. He was not only a doctor, an author, and principal of an experimental school, he was a champion for young Jews. Upon visiting a *Kibbutz* (a collective farm or settlement), he became certain that all Jews should move to Palestine. After the Germans occupied Warsaw, the orphanage was moved inside the ghetto. Korczak refused to wear the Star of David and was thrown into jail for a period for his actions. After the Warsaw Ghetto had been closed, Korczak and his family were taken to the Treblinka extermination camp. There, Korczak refused offers to escape and died with his children in the gas chambers. Today, many books have been written about him, and many of his own books and poetry have been translated into a host of different languages.

Hannah Senesh (Jewish) 1921-1944

At the age of 22, Hannah Senesh, a native Hungarian, joined the British army and began training to parachute behind German lines in order to make contact with resistance groups. After spending three months with Tito's partisans in Yugoslavia, she made an unsuccessful attempt to sneak into Hungary. After months of torture, Senesh refused to wear a blindfold and stared straight into the eyes of her firing squad. Her spirit is captured in a poem she wrote while in Yugoslavia, *Blessed is the Match*. In 1950, Senesh's remains were taken to Israel and reinterred in the military cemetery located on Mount Herz. Senesh started to write a diary at the age of 13. Remarkably, she continued to write it until shortly before her death.

Mordecai Anielewicz (Jewish) 1920-1943

Commander of the Warsaw Ghetto uprising, Mordecai Anielewicz was born into a poor family in a poor neighbourhood. After the Nazis declared war on Poland, he escaped the country for Romania, but returned to the Warsaw Ghetto in 1940 to organize a resistance. On April 19, 1943, Anielewicz and his ghetto fighters, armed only with 2 machine guns, 500 pistols, and 15 rifles, open fired on the German soldiers. The Germans took heavy casualties until they set buildings ablaze. People fleeing from the fire were taken to Treblinka. On May 8, the Germans used poison mustard gas to flush out the remaining fighters. About 100 people escaped through the sewers. Anielewicz was killed by the gas.

Vladka Meed (Jewish) 1923-

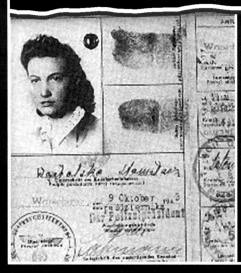

A member of the Jewish Fighting Organization of Warsaw, Vladka Meed lived outside the ghetto amongst the Poles in order to secure weapons for the resistance. She convinced non-Jews that she was not Jewish and using false identification papers Meed managed to smuggle weapons across the Warsaw Ghetto walls. She also smuggled people out of the ghetto and found places for them to hide. Through setting fire to German factories, building Molotov cocktails and collecting arms, Meed and her cohorts resisted the Nazis. After the liquidation of the ghetto, Meed continued to work for the Polish underground. Meed is now the director of the Holocaust and Jewish Resistance Summer Fellowship Program in Israel.

Simon Wiesenthal (Jewish) 1908-2005

Simon Wiesenthal was born in Buczacz, in the Ukraine. When the Nazis attacked the Soviets, he and his wife were sent to several labour camps. After 1942, when the Final Solution was implemented, Wiesenthal survived several death camps, a death march to Mauthausen, and was liberated just as he was on the brink of death. After the war, Wiesenthal worked tirelessly at gathering information to convict war criminals. After the Nuremberg trials he became a Nazi hunter and was responsible for bringing many war criminals to justice, including the notorious Adolf Eichmann. Wiesenthal was an author, and the most proud founder of the Simon Wiesenthal Center and the Museum of Tolerance. He died on September 21, 2005.

Sabina Zimering (Jewish) 1923-

Sabina Zimering, a Polish Jew, was 16 when World War II broke out. She spent three years hiding from the Nazis after the Gestapo raided her hometown of Piotrkow, Poland, in 1942. False IDs supplied by Catholic childhood friends saved her and her sister from the gas chambers of Treblinka. They survived as Catholic Poles in Nazi Germany working at a Gestapo hotel. After the war Sabina attended Munich Medical School, received her degree, emigrated to Minneapolis, and practiced medicine for 42 years. She began writing a memoir of her Holocaust experience when she retired from a career in medicine in 1996. Zimering's Holocaust Memoir *Hiding in the Open* became a Radio Talking Book for the Blind and a stage play at a local history theatre.

Henry Oertelt (Jewish) 1920-

Henry Oertelt was born in Berlin. His family escaped the Nazis until 1943, when he was sent to a series of camps including Auschwitz. Oertelt describes his survival of the Holocaust as a series of links in a chain. If one link had broken he would not have survived. Oertelt survived several death camps, including Auschwitz, and was finally liberated from Flossenburg while on a death march. He attributes his survival to many links, including unexpected kindness from people, being of small physical stature, having carpentry skills, and for keeping an optimistic outlook, despite the grave conditions. Henry and his wife Inge live in Minnesota, where he has written his memoirs, *An Unbroken Chain: My Journey through the Nazi Holocaust.*

Oskar Schindler (Ethnic German) 1908-1974

An ethnic German, Schindler was born April 28, 1908, in Zwittau, Austria-Hungary, what is now Moravia in the Czech Republic. He used the war as an opportunity to make a profit by acquiring a factory and using Jewish slave labour. What is miraculous about this story is that for some reason Schindler helped 1,300 Jews from his factory survive deportations and extermination. There are questions as to how much Schindler was involved with the "list", but as one Schindler Jew said, "I don't know what his motives were... What's important is that he saved our lives". Schindler died in 1974, alone and penniless. A book, *Schindler's List*, was written about his life, and was made into an Oscar-winning film by the Jewish-American director Steven Spielberg in 1993.

GLOSSARY

Allies The nations allied against the Axis powers during World War II, primarily Great Britain, France, the Soviet Union, and the United States.

Axis 1936 alliance of Germany and Italy that opposed the Allies in World War II. It later included Japan and other nations.

Anti-Semitism Hatred of and discrimination against Jews.

Aryan In Nazi racial theory, a person of pure German "blood". The term "non-Aryan" was used to designate Jews, part-Jews and others of supposedly inferior racial stock.

Chancellor Chief (prime) minister of Germany.

Concentration camp Prisons used without regard to accepted norms of arrest and detention.

Death camp Nazi extermination centres where Jews and other victims were brought to be killed as part of Hitler's Final Solution.

Death marches Forced marches of prisoners over long distances and under intolerable conditions was another way victims of the Third Reich were killed.

Dehumanization The Nazi policy of taking away the things that make a person an individual like their name, home, pets and freedoms.

DP Displaced Person. People who have nowhere to go after a war.

Displaced Persons Act of 1948 Law passed by U.S. Congress limiting the number of Jewish displaced persons who could emigrate to the United States.

Einsatzgruppen Mobile killing squads formed to follow the German army as they conquered land in Eastern Europe and murdered the Jews.

Euthanasia Deliberate killings of institutionalized physically, mentally, and emotionally handicapped people.

Final Solution A Nazi euphemism for the plan to exterminate the Jews of Europe.

Führer Meaning "Leader". Adolf Hitler's title in Nazi Germany.

Gas chambers Large chambers in which people were executed by poison gas.

Genocide The deliberate and systematic destruction of a racial, political, cultural or religious group.

Gestapo Acronym for *Geheime Staatspolizei*: Secret State Police. The Gestapo used brutal methods to investigate and suppress resistance to Nazi rule within Germany.

Ghettos Usually established in the poor sections of a city, most of the Jews from the city were forced to live here often surrounded by barbed wire or walls.

Goebbels, Paul Joseph Reich Propaganda Director of the NSDAP and Reich Minister of Public Enlightenment and Propaganda.

Gypsies A collective term for Romani and Sinti. A nomadic people believed to have come originally from northwest India.

***Hitler Jugend* / Hitler Youth** A Nazi youth group established in 1926. It expanded during the Third Reich. Membership was compulsory after 1939.

Holocaust The systematic planned extermination of about six million European Jews and millions of others by the Nazis between 1941-1945.

International Military Tribunal Court which prosecuted Nazi war criminals.

Kristallnacht Meaning "The Night of Broken Glass". On this night, November 9, 1938, almost 200 synagogues were destroyed; over 8,000 Jewish shops were ransacked and looted; and tens of thousands of Jews were removed to concentration camps.

Lebensraum Meaning "living space", it was a basic principle that more space was needed for Aryan Germans.

Majdanek Nazi camp and killing centre opened near Lublin in eastern Poland in late 1941.

Mein Kampf Meaning "My Struggle", was published in two volumes, vol. 1 in 1925 and vol. 2 in 1926, this work detailed Hitler's radical ideas of nationalism, anti-semitism, and Social Darwinism.

Mengele, Dr. Josef Senior SS physician at Auschwitz-Birkenau from 1943-44. One of the physicians who carried out the "selections" of prisoners upon arrival at camp. He also carried out cruel experiments on prisoners.

Nazi Party (National Socialist German Workers' Party) Founded in Germany in February, 1920, its platform was based on militaristic, racial, anti-semitic and nationalistic policies.

Nuremberg Laws The Nuremberg Laws were announced by Hitler at the Nuremberg Party conference, defining "Jew" and systematizing and regulating discrimination and persecution.

Pogrom An organized and often officially encouraged massacre of, or attack on, Jews.

Propaganda Information used to sway the opinions of the population.

Reich German word for empire.

Reichstag The German Parliament.

SA (Sturmabteilung or Storm Troopers) Also known as "Brownshirts", they were the Nazi party's main instrument for undermining democracy and facilitating Adolf Hitler's rise to power.

Shtetl A small Jewish town or village in Eastern Europe.

Sobibór Extermination camp located in the Lublin district of eastern Poland.

Sonderkommando the Jewish slave labour units in extermination camps that removed the bodies of those gassed for cremation or burial.

SS (Schutzstaffel / Protective Squadron) Hitler's personal guard. It was first formed in 1923 as a company of storm troopers charged with protecting Nazi leadership, although it was re-formed in 1925, following disbandment after the failed 1923 Putsch. From 1929, under Himmler, the SS developed into the most powerful affiliated organization of the Nazi party.

Der Stürmer Anti-semitic newspaper founded by Julius Streicher.

Swastika An ancient symbol used by the Nazis as their emblem.

Synagogue Jewish house of worship.

Third Reich Meaning "third regime or empire", the Nazi designation of Germany and its regime from 1933-45.

Treaty of Versailles A peace treaty signed by the Allies and Germany at the end of World War I. The Treaty forced the Germans to accept responsibility for World War I.

Wannsee Conference January 20, 1942, on a lake near Berlin. The occasion when SS official, Reinhard Heydrich, helped present and coordinate the Final Solution.

Weimar Republic The German republic which was an experiment in democracy (1919-1933), established after the end of World War I.

Zyklon-B (Hydrogen cyanide) Pesticide used in some of the gas chambers at the death camps.

INDEX

ACKNOWLEDGEMENTS

PICTURE CREDITS:

Every effort has been made to trace the copyright holders, and we apologise in advance for any unintentional ommissions. We would be pleased to insert the appropriate acknowledgements in any subsequent edition of this publication.

B=bottom; C=centre; L=left; R=right; T=top

Alamy: 6b, 7t, 18b, 22 all, 23t. Art Archive: 5b, 8b, 9r, 19cr, 32-33 all.
Corbis: 5r, 7b, 9t, 10b, 12b, 13b, 25c, 16cl, 27 all, 30-31 all, 35t, 37b, 38 all.
Everett Collection: 35b. United States Holocaust Memorial Museum: 2, 24b, 25b, 16t, 18l, 20t, 20b, 21b, 23cr, 26 all, 27 all, 36b.